BREAKING OUT
THE JAIL I BUILT

BREAKING OUT
THE JAIL I BUILT

By
Ebony A.N. Smith

CONFESSIONS
PUBLISHING

ACKNOWLEDGMENT

O H MY GOSH!!! This is so unreal. I cannot believe all those who have supported me throughout my life are reading my very first book. I just want everyone who accepted me just as I am to know that I love you so much from the very bottom of my heart, and I thank you.

To my mother Sandra B. I thank you for keeping your foot on my neck, and never letting me get too lost. You supported me through every obstacle I went through in life and stayed in my corner. Mama, I could never repay you for all that you have done for me.

Thank you so much to my dear friend, Natema for all the many days and nights you would pray with me, and for me. You are the definition of what a real friend is. I will forever cherish your support, and the way you always do things from your heart. God knew what he was doing when he placed you in my life.

To my two best chicks, Camerin and Shalamonèt, you two ladies always told me enough is enough, and reminded me that I was always so much better than my circumstances. You encouraged me to get grounded, let the past go, and move forward with grace, dignity, and pride. I thank you two for your constant encouragement. I probably would have never had the courage to write this book without you ladies cheering me on along the way.

This has been one wild ride, but, God, I thank you for every experience because it made me the woman I am today.

The day the Lord gave Frank Wildridge his wings, I know for a fact he helped God protect me every day of my life. He is and will always be my guardian angel. I love you always and forever, cousin. Continue to fly high and show up when and where you are needed.

CONTENTS

INTRODUCTION

INTRODUCTION

Thank you all for taking the opportunity to read my story. I am so grateful to be able to share my story with you. While this story is based on my life's events, I changed the names of the characters in the book because I am not telling their story but showcasing how each character impacted where I am today.

You will be able to see how the things that I have gone through in my life have allowed me to discover my purpose, and break free of what kept me locked up. I needed to take accountability, and know that I was the one who held the keys to my freedom. My purpose is to be as transparent as possible. I want to provide encouragement and empower women who have had the same experiences, or are having the same experiences as I did. I want to let them know they can overcome those experiences and stand in their purpose as well. All they must do is realize they hold the keys to their freedom.

Your crown may have fallen, but it did not break. Pick that beautiful crown up and place it back on top of your beautiful head. It may not be easy, and might even be a little heavy at first, but always remember the Queen that you are. Now fly free bird, fly.

LAYING THE FOUNDATION

CHAPTER 1

LAYING THE FOUNDATION

So it was, I had found the man of my dreams. Santiago, the man that I would spend the rest of my life with. We shared seven magnificent years together. Growing stronger, building a foundation, and making plans for our future. In the blink of an eye all of that came crashing down.

It was a real cool Saturday afternoon in October. Santiago had left for work at 2 pm as he does every day. My girlfriend Camila came over for our usual smoke session. When she got to my house, I was preparing dinner. As she is rolling the weed, I am cooking; we are laughing, having a great conversation, and reflecting on our day. In preparing dinner, I had made it to that point where I could step away from the stove, and let the food cook itself. We stepped outside on the porch to have a cigarette. Now, everybody and their mama was able to smoke all the weed they wanted in my house, but cigarettes were an absolute no-no. Those things got smoked outside.

So, Camila and I are outside smoking and I thought I saw a car just like the one Santiago drives pull through my gate. Turns out it was Santiago. My first thought is "What is this man doing here? It is only 5:30 pm. He is not supposed to be home until close to midnight." Santiago pulls up right in front of the house and just sits there. He is sitting there not doing a damn thing but staring at me with this dumb look on his face. I started getting nervous because he was looking nervous, and serious—almost scared. I immediately thought he either lost his job, or someone had died.

I began to walk towards the car to ask what was going on, I could not make it there fast enough because Santiago just drove off. "Oh, hell NO!!" I said so loud. I looked at Camila and started walking towards her, and once I got to her I said, "Girl, watch my food, I'll be back!" I ran in the house, grabbed my keys, and went and hopped in my car because I was going to find Santiago.

I did not make it too far before I spotted Santiago parked in the store parking lot, right around the corner from our house. I aggressively hopped out my car and snatched the passenger side door of Santiago's car open. "Dude, what's up?" I say frantically. Santiago is just sitting there crying uncontrollably. I then change my tone, since I see that he is crying. I then say, "Baby, what's wrong with you?" Through Santiago's tears and weeping voice, he says "Ebony, I have chlamydia!"

Now, I know I had not been unfaithful, so I was immediately filled with rage, hurt, and absolute confusion. I told Santiago we needed to return to the house so that we could talk.

By the time we got to the house, Camila had completed my dinner, and by the looks on Santiago's and my face, she knew that whatever was going on was not good. Wanting to give us the space that we needed at that moment, she told me she was going to go ahead and head out, and she would catch up with me later.

I had questions, I needed answers. I could not understand why, with all that Santiago had at home, he would go out and cheat on me. Not only to cheat, but to be so reckless and bring home a disease. Of course, he came with some sad a** bulls***. I had never had an STD in my life. I was not having any signs of an STD. No foul smells, no discharge, no itching—no nothing, but I felt absolutely disgusting.

First thing Monday morning, I called the doctor's office and explained to them what Santiago had shared with me, and they scheduled me an appointment the same day. I went in and had every STD screening there is. Santiago has chlamydia, so my doctor treated me for chlamydia without even having my test results back. Not only did they give me medicine, but they gave me a prescription for my partner as well. They said it was protocol for them to do that. Never ever did I stop to think, "Why didn't they give him medicine at the doctor when they told him? Since it is protocol for them to give you medicine for your partner, why hadn't Santiago provided me with a dose of medication to cure this mess?"

The next couple of days in my home were like a bad storm. It was gloomy. I was so sad. I was so angry. I was going apeshit at any given moment, just trying to process what I had just learned, while still trying to get through my everyday life.

When I went to the doctor, the doctor did tell me that I would only hear from them if my test results came back positive. With me not hearing anything from the doctor's office by that Thursday, I decided to give them a call. When I called, the receptionist told me that she would not be able to give me my test results, but she would be able to get me over to an advice nurse who would be able to deliver those results to me. Once the advice nurse was on the phone, I explained to her the reason for my phone call. She pulled up my chart and began to read off my results: "Your HIV test is negative, syphilis is negative, herpes is negative, chlamydia and gonorrhea are negative." I was so shocked and excited that I was not being affected by Santiago's little dirty ways. I shared my results with him, and he seemed very relieved, but he was still walking around looking stupid and sad. I agreed that this was not something that I thought should end our relationship. He made a mistake and I forgave him.

But that was not good enough for Santiago. He was still walking around looking dumb, stupid, and sad, every day. My thoughts were, "It is not the end of the world. Just take the little stupid pills, YOUR chlamydia will be gone, and we can move on with our lives!" Boy, were my thoughts wrong.

That following Saturday, my mom and I decided that we had not visited with my grandfather in a while, so we decided to take a little road trip down to Oakland, CA, where he and his wife lived. We headed out early Saturday morning and spent a perfect day in the bay area catching up with my grandfather. We ate good, laughed, talked, and just really had a good day. The whole day had gone by, and now it was time for my mom and I to head back to Sacramento. Mom and I went back and forth about who was going to drive us home. I ended up convincing her that she should drive.

We got home at about 10:30 that night, and boy, was I tired. Santiago and I still were not in a good place. When I walked in, I saw him sitting in the living room playing his Xbox, and with total disgust in my voice I said, "hey", and proceeded to my bedroom. I changed my clothes and got straight into bed. After being in bed for about ten minutes, here comes Santiago's ass walking through the bedroom door. He takes a seat at the foot of the bed. The same side that I was laying on.

He then spoke the words that took the life out of my body:

"Ebony, I'm HIV Positive."

I sprung out of bed and onto my feet. I started running, screaming, and crying so loud that you would have thought someone died. In my mind, I was a dead woman walking. Santiago was going to die soon. I thought: "Why God? Why me?"

I had not shared with my mother what had happened the week prior, but at this point, I had no choice but to call her. I felt like I was drowning—totally suffocating. Being the supportive mother that she is, she ran to my aid, and was at my house in ten minutes. That ten minutes seemed like forever.

After things had settled a tad bit, Santiago told me that he never had chlamydia; hence, the reason why, when I was tested, my chlamydia test came back negative. He only told me that he had chlamydia so that I would go to the doctor and get tested. Santiago had a follow up appointment the following week, and said, since my HIV test came back negative, he needed me to support him through his next doctors visit. I did not want to hear none of that. I wanted to murder this man, bust his head wide open; but I had to think, "This man just told me he is HIV positive, so I can't have his sick blood all over my damn house!" Life as I knew it had completely come to a halt. I was stuck in a time warp. All I could think was, "I'm getting ready to die, and I'm going to die a slow agonizing death. Lord, why me?"

Monday morning, I am frantically calling my doctor to be seen again, so I can be tested again. To remind you, the HIV test I had taken a week earlier had come back negative. My doctor explained that they usually do not give HIV tests back to back, but she could see and could feel how distraught I was, so she agreed to do it. The second test came back negative as well. My doctor explained that when she got my results back for the chlamydia, and it was negative, she was confused because chlamydia is not a disease you can have, and your partner does not have. That is a one in a trillion chance. She was disappointed in Santiago because she said that if he had told me right away, there would have been a cocktail she could have given me to prevent the virus from attacking my blood cells. Because he did not tell me, I now had to wait eighteen months to be sure that I did not have it, and I had to be tested every ninety days for the first six months, and every six months thereafter.

I ended up going to the doctor's appointment with Santiago. I needed to know what his doctor had to say. While at the appointment, the doctor talked about his viral load, t-cell count, how much technology there is now, the medication that they have for those infected, how Santiago and I could still have a normal life, and still have children. None of it made sense to me one bit. When we initially got into Santiago's appointment, Santiago told his doctor that he could share all his medical information with me. During the appointment, Santiago's doctor made a comment about him having full blown AIDS, and how to bring his status to HIV. Another lie this man told me. At the time, I did not know the difference, I just knew AIDS sounded worse than HIV.

I was so confused. I did not know which way was up or down, left or right, forward or backwards. I knew I was not dead yet, so I still had to keep pressing forward. Still had to work, still had to eat, still had to pay my bills, but, baby, when I tell you I was moving like a programmed robot, understand, I went through every day with no thoughts or emotions. No blood running through my veins. My heart even stopped beating at times (I think).

Santiago stayed in our home dealing with his stuff, and with his depression for a little over a month after the news had broke. During that time, I drove myself more insane than I already was. I did not want Santiago in my kitchen swinging my refrigerator open. I did not want Santiago using the same toilet as me. I was scared to leave my toothbrush in the bathroom. I was very uneducated on the virus, and the whole ordeal made me a nervous wreck.

Now, of course, after learning that Santiago had the incurable virus, I opted not to stay in a relationship with him. Me seeing the man I love face the reality of having to start his life over was hard on me. I allowed him to stay until he came up with a plan as to how he was going to proceed with his new life. He moved out of state, which was the best thing for him and I. He did not want to face the embarrassment from his family and friends, and I was continually contemplating how I was going to get away with murdering Santiago for ruining my life as I knew it.

THE BARBED

WIRE FENCE

CHAPTER 2

THE BARBED WIRE FENCE

While Santiago and I were together, I worked at a local sales company. I had been there a few months before this lady named Lucia started working there. Nobody in the office liked Lucia when she started. They felt like she was stuck up, and they said she thought she was too cute and better than everybody. I am nice to everybody until you personally do something that I do not like. I did not have the same reservations about Lucia as everyone else. Lucia and I became incredibly good friends. Lucia was six years my senior, so she had experienced life a little bit more than I had. I would share my personal stories and experiences with her, and she would share the same. She had her man and I had mine.

When Lucia and I first started hanging out, I noticed that she would stare at me. Just stare and look me so deep in my eyes, it was as if she were trying to snatch my soul. It took a while, but I finally understood why she would look at me so deeply.

We were having a conversation about ex-lovers, and she was sharing a story about somebody she had dated years ago. Turns out this person she was talking about was a woman. Me being shocked and surprised, I was like, "Girl, you gay?" She said, "Noooo, I'm not gay. I'm bi-sexual!", in a real seductive voice. She went on to tell me how much she enjoyed being touched by a woman. I could not relate. I had never looked at a woman like that, nor had any kind of sexual feelings or attraction.

As time went on, Lucia and I grew closer. We were hanging out a lot more. The deep stares became more frequent. I was starting to become attracted to this woman. There was no man around showing me all the attention that she was. I was being turned out and did not even realize it. I finally came out and told Lucia that I wanted to experience being with a woman sexually. Of course, that was her plan all along.

During the last couple of months before Santiago moved out of state, Lucia and I spent a lot of time together. She was going through it with her man too. When I shared what was going on with Santiago and I, she was so supportive and attentive. She was always available when I needed to vent. Always available to keep me company, to go out on outings with me, to go shopping, to get our nails done, for girl's night out, having fun, and getting drunk. Lucia and Hennessy were my new best friends.

One weekend after Santiago and I split, Lucia invited me to spend the weekend with her. I did not want to be home alone, so I took her up on her offer. Her man was in jail, so it was just her and I at her house. That Saturday we went out and shopped. I got a few knickknacks for the house and went to the grocery store. Lucia was so hospitable. She set me up real comfortably in her room with dim lights, candles, and the remote to find a good movie. She made the most delicious dinner for us. Dungeness crab, shrimp, rice with this bomb ass butter sauce, and salad. She finished her food before I did, and when she was done, she went and ran me a bath. Talk about putting the moves on me right. My bath had bubbles, bath bombs, oils, and candles. It was a total escape from my current reality. I went and sat in that bathtub for about 30 minutes before Lucia came in to check on me. She came in and kneeled at the side of the bathtub and asked for my towel as she picked up the soap. She lathered up that towel good, and gently began to wash my back. It felt so good. Once she was done, she handed me the towel and I finished washing the rest of my body. When I got out, Lucia got in. I was a little nervous because all I could think was, "OMG, is this really happening?" I was thinking so many different things, but whatever was going to happen that night, I was ready for it.

I put on my gown and got in the bed while Lucia finished her shower. When Lucia got out the shower, I watched her dry and lotion her body. Once she was done, without putting on anything, she came and got in the bed with me. It was at that moment that I had my first sexual experience with a woman. Afterwards, I laid on her chest and fell right asleep. This was the first of the many sexual encounters Lucia and I shared.

Lucia's boyfriend soon got out of jail, and when he got out, Lucia and I did not spend as much time together as we did when he was locked down, but we still talked often. I was still going through the agony of waiting for the next 18 months.

Even though Lucia was not around, I still had my girl Camila who would come over and hang out with me every single day after work. It became the new normal to get up every day, get ready for work, put the thought of the possibilities out of my mind, get through the work day, get off work, stop at the liquor store to grab a bottle, and meet Camila at my house so we could smoke weed until we couldn't get high anymore. Wake up and do it all over again.

My whole life I was a chunky girl, but the worry of the unknown left me with absolutely no appetite. Within three months of the news breaking, I had lost 50 lbs. I was skinnier than I had ever been in my whole entire life. When people would see me that I had not seen in a while, they would tell me how good I looked, and be totally amazed that I had lost so much weight. They had no idea of the stress that I was carrying. I would smile and just say, "Thank you." I had become good at faking it for the public.

I had rapidly lost so much weight, I was certain that I was sick. Three months had gone by since Santiago told me about his HIV status, and it was time for me to have my first blood drawn. Walking into that laboratory felt as if I was walking to the electric chair. I sat down in the chair, and while I waited for the phlebotomist to get ready to draw my blood, I prayed and prayed as I had been doing. She poked me with that needle, and as I watched my blood shoot up into that test tube, I was saddened by the thought of a possible positive result. The next few days left me worried. I had not heard from the doctor with my results, so I called them scared out of my mind, only for them to deliver the results as negative. The doctor had not called me because there was nothing wrong.

Whew, that was one test down with three more to go. While I should have been excited, I was still worried and stressed out because the doctors were clear that they could not be certain until 18 months after my first test. I could not help but worry. Outside of working, and drinking, and smoking, I read as much literature as I could get my hands on when it came to the HIV/AIDS virus. I learned how it was transmitted. I learned about the white and red blood cell count. Learned about what it meant to be undetectable, and a host of other things. I learned that I could not get it from sharing dishes, or using the same toilet as a person who is infected with the virus. Once the virus hits the air, it dies. I did so much research because of the possibility of how this could affect my life.

After the first results were negative, Camila and I celebrated big time at my house, smoking, drinking, eating, and talking. While we were celebrating, I shared with Camila my girl on girl experience, without going into detail. Immediately her response was she wanted to try it. When we were talking, she and I were sitting on my living room couch, and without wasting any time, Camila kneeled down in front of me and went to work. All I could think was, "There is no way this woman has never done this before."

Camila and I were already hanging out every day, but after we had sex, the dynamics of our relationship changed. To the public eye, it appeared we were the best of friends, but as time went on, and we were alone, we grew closer intimately. We had a "secret" love affair that only her and I knew about. At that time, she was everything I needed. My companion and the reason I smiled every day.

Another three months had passed by, and it was time for me to take my fourth HIV test. I had the same feelings and emotions when walking into that laboratory and watching my blood enter that test tube. Again, the doctor's office had not called with my results, so I called them with worry on my mind. Again, the results were negative. I was thanking GOD, but still worried. I did not have the mindset I have now. You cannot pray and worry at the same time.

I began to get happy about life again. After the fourth test, the doctor explained that since it had been six months since I had been exposed to the virus, she could almost guarantee that I hadn't transmitted the virus, and the next two tests would be precautionary. That was something else that did not make sense. I just knew I had a year to go before it was certain that I did not have it.

Six more months had gone by and I experienced the same feelings walking into that laboratory. I was scared while watching what could be HIV infected blood shoot up into that test tube. Same thing: no phone call from the doctor's office with the results, so I called them to give me a negative result yet again.

Now I was in my final stretch of testing. I had one more test to take and be negative, and I would know I was in the clear. I had made it to my sixth and last HIV test. I had the same feelings walking into the laboratory the last four times. Same thing happened: the doctor's office did not call me, so I called them. This time when I called to get my results, it was a lot different.

I was at work on my lunch break when I called to get my results. I knew the receptionist could not deliver my results, so I immediately asked to be transferred to an advice nurse. Once on the phone with the advice nurse, I explained to her the reason for my call. This time the advice nurse told me she could not give me my results over the phone, but that she wanted to schedule an appointment to come into the office for my doctor to give me my results face to face. Immediately I lost what little life I had left in my body. I began to panic and cry so hard. I just knew with her telling me that she could not give me the results that the results had to be positive. I went back and forth with her about how I was given my results over the phone in the past and needed to know what made this time any different. She explained how laws had changed, and they just did not give those results over the phone anymore. I did not believe her. I told her I was not waiting on no damn appointment; I was on my way to the doctor's office at that very moment.

I went to my manager in a panic and told her that I had a family emergency and had to leave for the day. I was so scared at that moment. I left my job and have no idea how I made it to the doctor's office. It was like I was not driving. I did not see any cars on the road, no traffic lights—no nothing. I walked into that doctor's office already knowing my fate. I gave the receptionist my name and told her the reason why I was there in a panic. She asked me to calm down and have a seat while she went to get the nurse. I could not sit. I could not stop shaking. The nurse who I had just got off the phone with came to the door where they called you back to see the doctor, and said, "Ebony Smith." I hurried over to the door, she had already heard the worry in my voice over the phone, and now she could see the worry on my face. When I got to the door, her words to me were, "Ebony, your results came back NEGATIVE!"

I never knew what it was like to feel your knees buckle, but at that moment I had no feet, knees, or legs. I began to fall to the floor, luckily the nurse caught me in her arms. I cried tears of absolute joy and disbelief. I was so mad that they made me go through all those emotional changes that day. I could not thank God enough for sparing my life. God said, "Not my child!!"

THE CONCRETE

WALLS

CHAPTER 3

THE CONCRETE WALLS

Camila and I were still hanging strong, and I felt so renewed. I had just gone through a horrible break up. Spent the last 18 months of my life constantly worrying. I had not had any male interaction as far as dating goes since Santiago and I had split. I was ready for some male company.

I started dating Matias. Matias was quite the charmer. He was that good dark chocolate, had the most beautiful smile, and when I say he could dress his butt off, I mean he was always sharp and dressed to the T. He was also so hilarious, kept me rolling with uncontrollable laughter. Matias did all the things I liked to do. We smoked, drank, and partied hard. He was not my man, but every weekend you would have sure thought he was. We were together every Friday and Saturday night.

Camila and I had gone out one Saturday night and had an absolute ball. Matias was there at the club that night, and he and I made plans to hook up afterward. I drove to the club that night, and Camila rode with me. After the party was over, I dropped Camila off at home, and I proceeded to go meet Matias. Matias and I decided to meet up at his cousin's house. As I was driving over to his cousin's, I fixed my makeup and hair. I am sure I was speeding at the same time.

When I arrived at Matias cousin's house, the party had not stopped just because the club had closed. There were a lot of people at Matias's cousin's house. Smoking, drinking, playing cards, and dominos—just still having a good time. Matias and I had snuck off to the back room so we could be alone.

After being there for about 30 minutes, there was a knock on the door, an unusual banging. Matias and I did not know who it was, this was not our house, so we kept on talking and doing what we were doing. Shortly after I heard Matias's cousin call out my name. I responded, and when I responded, that let his cousin know where I was in his house, so he came to the bedroom door and opened it and he said, "Eb, the police are here for you." I thought he was joking, but I was sadly mistaken.

Someone had followed me all the way to Matias's cousin's house because they suspected I was driving under the influence of alcohol. They called the police, and the police came to Matias's cousin's house. When the police got there, they told Matias's cousin that they needed the owner of the car that I had at the time to come out of the house. Well, Matias's cousin told the police that he did not know who drove that car.

Weed wasn't legal at the time, so the police told Matias's cousin that if the owner of my vehicle didn't come out, then they were coming in to search the place because they smelt weed. Matias' cousin, nor anybody in that house, wanted those kind of problems. So, I told Matias's cousin to tell them that I am not there, and he explained that he already did, and what their response was.

I went ahead and went outside. The police explained to me why they were there. I was nervous as shit, as I had never been in contact with the law, outside of being pulled over for a traffic ticket. The police told me they wanted to do a field sobriety test on me. At that point I knew I was going to jail because I was full of liquor. Everybody who was inside of Matias's cousin's house had made their way outside to observe. I was so embarrassed. I passed all their little field sobriety tests with no problem, but they still wanted me to blow in that little machine. I blew in the machine and blew a .14. I had never been to jail, but I was on my way that night.

I was arrested for the first time in my life for driving under the influence. I was scared yet again. I thought jail was like what I had seen on TV. That was just TV though. TV gives jail some credit. Sacramento County jail was the worst place I had ever been in my entire life. It's dirty. It stinks. The police were so mean to you, I mean it was just horrible. Luckily, I did not have to dress in jail clothes, or be transferred to the upstairs part of the jail. They booked and held me for 14 hours in the holding tank.

After being released it was determined that I would do no jail time, but I would pay a large fine, have my driver's license suspended, and go to a three-month DUI program. You would have thought that was enough to sit my butt down, but nope, I kept it up.

Matias ended up moving back to the bay area where he was originally from, and we started seeing less of each other. My daily routine stayed the same: work, get off work, smoke—and drinking a whole lot more. Even though I was handling my business daily, I was self-destructing like nobody's business.

SECURING THE ROOF

CHAPTER 4

SECURING THE ROOF

I t was time for my favorite cousin's baby shower. Everybody in the family was showing up and showing out to welcome her first child into the world. Her mother had invited all her close friends to the shower as well.

Back in the day, baby showers used to be for women only, but in this day a lot more baby showers are now co-ed. Seeing as how Camila and I were inseparable, she attended the baby shower with me. My aunt's friend ended up coming to the baby shower with her tall, strong, handsome son, Javier. When Javier and I met, we instantly clicked. It was like love at first sight. Even though we were at a party with a ton of other people, it was like him and I were the only ones there. Camila had an attitude because I was so engulfed in this man, but that did not bother me one bit. Javier and I exchanged numbers that day before leaving the party, and I had no idea our relationship was going to just take off after that.

Javier lived and worked in the bay area, and I lived in Sacramento, but Javier was making it a point to get to Sacramento every day after work and on the weekends, he wanted to spend every moment with me. We had so much in common. We both liked to drink, number one. We liked the same music. We liked the same movies. We liked the same foods. Our families were linked in. It was like a match made in heaven. Javier and I spent so much time together that I did not have much time for Camila. I had a man now, and it felt so much better than what I was used to.

Javier and I were about three months into our relationship, one day I got a call from some woman named Felisha claiming to be Javier's girlfriend/baby mama. She had questions about where, when, and why, I was messing with her man that had been her man for the last 15 years. I was so confused as to why this lady was on my phone talking about HER man, who had been with me every day for the last three months. When I was not with him, and he was away working, I was constantly on the phone with him.

Felisha claimed that he and her had been on a break, but now he was back home, so she wanted me to stop talking to him. Well, this very same day Javier was on the highway on the way to my house, so I did not call him right away because I had to think about what just happened. I waited until he got to my house so we could talk face to face.

Of course, when he got there, we had the opportunity to talk, and his response to Felisha's phone call of course was that she was lying. Yeah, that was his baby mama, but they had been broken up, and he did not want her, he wanted me. He did not just say it, but he showed it with his actions. He was still with me all the time. Felisha just would not let it go. She kept calling my phone, and kept calling his phone. She kept harassing us to the point that I could no longer take it. I opted to bow out gracefully and decided to break it off with Javier. My feelings were hurt, but it was a decision I had to make.

Although he ultimately ended up back with Felisha, she still would not leave me alone. When he would pull one of his disappearing acts, she would call me looking for him. Each time I became annoyed and would respond with, "Girl, what do you want? I sent your man back right into your arms. What more do you want from me? I am out of it!" It did not appear to me that she believed me because she would send me pictures, voice recordings, and videos of them together. Each time my response was the same, "Look lady, I do not care. You won." Even though I knew Felisha was tripping, I knew she was not lying about Javier and her relationship. There was some truth to what she was saying.

Two months after I called it quits with Javier, I found out he and Felisha got married at the courthouse. My feelings were so hurt by this news. But I have always been the kind of girl to just carry on, so I knew I would get over it.

But I was not able to just get over it as easily as I thought. Mainly because of Felisha. Even though she was married to him, Felisha wanted to rub in my face every chance she got that she not only got her baby's daddy back, but that she was now married to him. Although she did what she could to portray this picture-perfect marriage in an attempt to hurt me, it did not truly work. Javier was calling me even after they had gotten married.

Because Felisha would not let me move on, and continued to play with me, I decided I was going to show her once and for all.

One day I agreed to meet Javier after work. We met for dinner and drinks at Scotts on the River, and afterwards we went to the Citizens Hotel. We talked, took a nice bubble bath together, and made the sweetest love. I did not meet him because I missed him, or even wanted to see him. It was because I was determined that I was going to have the last laugh.

After we spent the night together, we parted ways. As revenge, I sent Felisha pictures, videos, and text messages from our night together. I did this to prove a point to her that he still wanted me. She could never be me! Instead of waiting for a reply from her, I blocked them both and carried on with my life.

INSTALLING THE BARS

CHAPTER 5

INSTALLING THE BARS

Seeing as how I had been spending so much time with Javier, Camila and I stopped hanging as much. The routine Camila and I had before I started seeing Javier had changed. Camila scored her a new boo during this time. Camila was living with her parents, but upon meeting this new guy, she decided she wanted to spread her wings and finally move out of her parents' house. Unlike Camila, I moved out of my parents' house as soon as I graduated from high school. I was 18 when I got my first apartment. I had been living on my own. Since my house had free range, Camila spent a lot of time there.

Camila found her an apartment, but also had a roommate to help her with half of the bills. I did not care for Camila's roommate because she was always trying to take Camila's time away from me. Camila knew it, and it seemed like she would purposely allow this to happen. It seemed as if she was trying to get me back because I left her hanging when I met Javier.

One day, I was over at Camila's new place and we had been drinking. Camila and I were chilling in her room with the door closed. She was unpacking at the time and I was helping her. She did not have a bed in her room, and there was a box that needed to be unpacked, so I decided I was going to unpack that box. Because there wasn't a bed or any chairs to sit on, my only option was to sit on the floor. I loudly flopped my body onto the floor. Not purposely, but because it was a long way down. Camila at this point aggressively told me that I needed to be mindful that she has a roommate, her roommate must be respected, and I cannot be making all this noise. I immediately became offended. This lady wanted to tell me how to behave in her house, when she would come to my house every single day and was made to feel at home. At that moment, an argument broke out, and we got loud. Louder than me plopping down on the floor for sure. She asked me to go ahead and just leave her house. I got even more upset and told her I was not going anywhere. She grabbed my shirt and tried to move me. This was the point things became physical. Things may have escalated, because we had been drinking.

We immediately started throwing blows at each other. The alcohol had me off all ten of my toes (meaning, I was unbalanced to say the least). We continued to swing our fists at each other until Camila suddenly threw a punch that hit me smack dab in my right eye. As a result of all the commotion that had been going on between the two of us, her roommate came into the room and separated the two of us from fighting. We separated, but not without continuing to make a scene. I made sure I was extremely loud as I was making my exit. I literally cussed and yelled all the way out the door and to my car. I decided at that moment I was not dealing with that lady anymore.

When I woke up the next morning, I was still feeling like fu** that bi***. I am not dealing with her anymore. I opened my home to her and as soon as she got a little piece of an apartment, this was how she treated me. Oh, I was done! That was until I walked in the bathroom and saw that my eye was black. I have light skin, and the whole part under my right eye was black and purple. I went from "Fu** that bi***" to I am about to fu** this bi*** up." This was the first time I had ever in my life had a black eye and I was not about to go out like that.

I called up my friends and told them what had happened, and they were ready to ride on Camila too. Later that night, me and two of my home girls went back over to Camila's house. When we got there my friends asked me if I wanted them to go in with me. I told them "No, that this was between her and I, and I am the only one who is about to rock her world!"

I made sure I was sober all day before going to Camila's. I was high on adrenaline alone. I got to Camila's door, and it appeared as if nobody was home, but I saw Camila's car outside, so I knew she was there. It was like I had the force of 10 men behind me because with my first try I kicked her front door open. I ran up the stairs leading to her bedroom, she heard me coming and she tried her hardest to close her room door before I reached it. I was ready to kick that door in if I had to, even if it had been closed and locked, but she was not quick enough. When I reached her, I commenced to whooping her ass. I gave Camila the business. I swear I made her touch every wall in her room. It lasted about five minutes before I realized the police may have been on their way. I had already decided I had gotten her good enough. I left Camila lying on the floor. Yes, she was breathing.

My girls were still outside waiting for me in the car. Once I reached them, I hopped in the passenger seat and we quickly drove off. Now that I got her back for blacking my eye, I was OK with "Fu** that bi***"

It was time for a drink. My girls and I celebrated big time over that victory that night. She was not just about to blacken my eye and get away with it. I went home that night and climbed into my bed and slept like a champ.

The next day Camila's brother decided that he wanted to call and threaten my life. He was enraged after seeing how I left his sister. He was doing all this threatening, but had no idea what was really going on between his sister and I. He did not know the truth about Camila and my relationship. As he made his many threats, I could not understand for the life of me why she would allow this man to call my phone. At this point, I had not involved any of my family or friends in our situation.

Once I got tired of hearing him talk, I had to break the truth down to him. He really needed to just stay in his own lane and mind his own business. I told him his sister and I were more than just friends. She was my girlfriend and we were on the down low (yes, women be on the down low too). I also told him he would never be able to understand where our anger came from. He was so shocked (as he should have been). This new revelation did not stop the threats at all, he still had his sister's back.

As a result of his continued threats, I had to call on everyone I knew that would have my back, including my mother. Because things had escalated so quickly, I was forced to reveal to my mother that Camila and I had been sexually involved. It did not matter though, my mama still was committed to being there for me.

The threats kept coming from Camila's brother. I decided to get a restraining order against Camila and her whole family. To get the restraining order, I had to face Camila and her family in domestic violence court given the nature of our relationship. Of course, Camila was way too ashamed to admit that we had been together sexually. Unlike her, I did not care who knew at this point. My mama was with me. She always told me she would support me as long as I was completely honest. My mama's support was all that mattered to me. I did not give a damn about what another soul knew about my life.

After everything had been finalized in court, I decided to move. I did not want Camila knowing where I lived. The best thing for me to do was move. Besides, I also had so many bad memories in that house with Santiago.

There was no more Santiago, no more Camila, no more Javier, and no more Felisha. I had moved into my new place and got hired on with the State. Life was turning around, and everything seemed to be turning around for the better. I now had a fresh start without baggage from the past.

This proved to be a perfect time for me and my old friend Lucia to re-connect. During this entire time, Lucia and I had not completely lost touch. It just so happened that Lucia and her boyfriend ended up splitting up as well. Now she and I were both single and ready to mingle. It was time to party.

Lucia did not live in Sacramento but would drive down every weekend so we could run the streets together. Unlike me, Lucia did not stay single for long. A new love, Ricardo, came into her life. He literally swept her off her feet.

Ricardo was the perfect match for her and had no issue with Lucia and my friendship. The amount of time she and I spent together did not bother him because he liked to party right along with us. He even paid for everything when we would step out.

Boy, did we have a blast together! At the time I had no idea how life as I now knew it would soon quickly change, and the change would all start by me hanging out with those two.

THE SURVEILLANCE

CHAPTER 6

THE SURVEILLANCE

It was Ricardo's cousin Diablo's birthday celebration. At the time, I had no idea that Diablo had just been released from prison. Well, that night was like an absolute movie. It started off by me leaving home and driving to the bay area to meet Lucia and Ricardo. I looked way too cute that night and was ready to party. I get to Oakland, park my car, and get in the car with Lucia and Ricardo. It was about 10 pm at that time. Lucia and Ricardo drove a minivan. The van had the first row of the back seat removed, so there was this big open space between the front seat and the back seat. The plan was for me to hook up with Ricardo's cousin Diablo and be his company for the evening. After I got into their van, our first stop was to pick up Diablo.

At first glance, Diablo was a certified riff-raff type of guy. He walked to the van looking so stupid; pants sagging down to the middle of his thigh, walking side to side, and he had on this chain that was almost bigger than him, and was swinging each direction his body was moving. When he got into the car, I immediately knew I was definitely not attracted to him, but because I came to have a good time, I pushed it aside.

That night we were headed towards a party at Lake Merritt. Once there, Lucia and Ricardo were inseparable all night. This left me with one of two options, get to know Diablo, or be alone. I decided to relax and get to know him. I was glad that I did because that night I learned Diablo loved to dance just as much as me. Once I found this out, he and I danced for hours. It was as if no one else was on the dance floor besides the two of us.

I was a dancing machine that night. When we left the party I was still dancing. Once in the van, I made my own dance floor where the middle row once was. I literally danced for the rest of our van ride.

We ended up in Cache Creek at the casino resort. While there, we won a few dollars before the night was over. When we left Cache Creek, I ended up falling asleep on the ride back. The whole ride I thought we were on our way back to the bay area. When I finally woke up, I was so discombobulated.

I was not at my car. Instead, I was at a Motel 6 in the middle of nowhere. I asked Lucia why were we there, she said because she was tired and could not drive back. Immediately I told her I would drive back. I needed to get home. Besides, I had no plans on being gone that night and the entire next day. I had things to do, and I did not know this Diablo character. I did not want to stay in a motel room with him. Of course, he would think because we were in a motel room together, we were going to have sex. I was not up to doing that with him.

Unbeknownst to me, Lucia had already booked two rooms before I had woken up. One for her and Ricardo, and the other for Diablo and me. I was so freaking pissed to say the least.

I was left with no other choice but to share the motel room with Diablo. Unsurprisingly, just like I had expected he wanted to have sex. I was not having it. I denied all of his advances. Because his attempts were futile, he finally fell asleep. He was completely knocked out. I laid there so disgusted by the fact that he tried to have sex with me, and that he was now snoring loudly.

After barely sleeping comfortably, I was ready to go. At about noon, Diablo and I left our room and headed to Lucia and Ricardo's room. Once there, I complained the entire time about how I was ready to go. Man, I was so irritated.

Despite my complaints, we did not end up leaving until about 4 pm that day. By the time I finally reached my car it was dawn. I was tired of being in any car at this point, but it was way past the time that I needed to get back to Sacramento. When I got to my car, they all knew how upset I was because I did not speak the whole ride back. To show it, when I got out of their van I did not say good-bye to anyone.

As soon as I get into my car and start it up, Diablo gets out of theirs and walks towards my car. Although I was still upset, I rolled down my window. He tells me how much of a good time he had and that he would love to hang out with me again soon. He asked for my number, and I gave it to him. Outside of all the unnecessary and unwanted time I spent out that night, I did have fun partying with him.

It took me just a little over an hour to get back to Sacramento. I was moving at the speed of lightning. I could not wait to get out of the two-day old clothes I had on, take a nice hot bath, and relax, because I had to be at work the next morning. Before going home, I had to stop and get me a bottle, of course. I had just been through a lot, and Henny was going to help me unwind.

I stopped at the liquor store by my house, and I noticed there was this ever so handsome man in the parking space next to me. He gets out and goes into the store. My only thought was, "Damn, he is fine as hell," but I was still looking like yesterday, so I just knew he was not going to be paying me any attention.

I got out of my car and walked into the store as if I were in a hurry. Suddenly, I heard the sexiest deepest voice say, "Is your husband in that truck?" I looked around the store because I just knew he was not talking to me, only to realize we were the only two people in the store. Shockingly, and so timidly, I responded, "I'm not married." He responded, "Well, my name is Flavio, and I would love to get to know you." Without even introducing myself properly, my goofy ass replied, "Sure!" He put my number in his phone and proceeded to ask me if my hair was real. I had long thick hair back then, and my curls were big and pretty. At this point, I was beyond flattered.

I was pushed over the edge when he told how beautiful I was, even complimented me on how pretty my hair was. I was now on cloud nine after receiving these compliments. I made my purchase and walked straight out of the store. While walking, cheesing ear to ear, lost in my thoughts, I heard him say, "You never told me your name." I said, "Oh sh**! I'm Ebony, it was nice to meet you, Flavio." To which he replied, "The pleasure is mine and I'll talk to you soon." What a great way to end my weekend.

For the next two weeks, I talked to Diablo every day. He kept up with me through phone calls and text messages. He wanted to hook up and take me out again. Even though I wasn't really feeling him like that initially, he somehow started to grow on me.

While conversing with Diablo, I was also having long conversations with Flavio. His voice was so seducing and sexy. I could talk to him for hours. Flavio and I had not seen each other since the night we met, aside from sending pictures back and forth. Although this was the case, I was really into him.

Just a short while after meeting Diablo, he ended up going to jail. He got sentenced to a year in San Quentin. Initially, I tried to keep the lines of communication open between he and I by writing and sending pictures. At the same time, I was still talking to Flavio.

During the course of us talking, Flavio ended up going out of state for about two weeks. Once he returned home, a relationship between us began to develop fast. As a result, I started returning Diablo's letters back to sender and stopped talking to him completely. I knew the jail life was not for me anyway. I cut him off cold turkey, he did not hear from me from that point forward.

I had Flavio, who I absolutely adored. And he adored and spoiled me. I did not need anything, but he would make sure I had everything I wanted. This made me fall for him even more. It was to the point that I liked just staring at him. I liked hearing him speak. I liked how he held his mouth, how he walked, and all the fun we would have together.

Things continued to progress quickly. After a short time of us dating, Flavio ended up moving in with me. Things were perfect between the two of us until Flavio started pulling these disappearing acts. By that time, we had only been together a few short months. During those times, he would disappear sometimes two days at a time. No call, no text—no nothing.

I had been down a similar road before, so I knew something was not right, even though he always had a good reason as to why he just went completely ghost. After the second disappearing act, I said, "oh, I am going to fix his a**."

At that time, Flavio had his own phone service, and I had mine. It just so happened Sprint had just released a new phone, so I upgraded my phone, and added him to my phone line. He was extremely happy because he had an ancient old school flip phone. The phones I got for us were the latest touchscreen phones.

Even though I was sweet on Flavio, I had not shared with him my past relationship experiences just yet. He had no idea that I had developed the skills of being a true investigator. His phone being on my account was going to answer a lot of my questions without me even having to ask him. I was able to see every single phone call and text that came to and from the phone. Not only that, but I was also able to locate him at any given moment. With the touch of a button, I was able to see his exact location.

One day everything was flowing just as it should. I went to work and had been talking to Flavio all throughout the day. After getting off, I went home and started preparing dinner. I called Flavio because there was something I needed from the store that I was hoping he could grab on his way home, but I got no answer. I waited about an hour to see if he would return my call. He did not call, so I called again. No answer. I immediately went to my locator and located him at a hospital. I got nervous and started calling like crazy. I even called the hospital. To my surprise they told me he was not a patient there. He was at that hospital all night until the next morning.

When he finally contacted me the next day, he apologized for not answering my calls. Flavio told me he was at the hospital all night with his friend who had gotten shot in the stomach. His excuse for staying all night was that the doctors were not sure if his friend was going to live. Flavio finished by telling me he was not going to be home that day but would be home the following day.

Even though I was very bothered that he didn't call me that night and explain all of this to me, I believed him because I could actually see on my locator that he was in fact at the hospital all night long. I did not see Flavio the next day, but on the locator, I could see that he was back up at that hospital. I just empathized and sympathized with him because his friend had just gotten shot, and he was sad.

The following day, he finally made it home and was waiting for me when I got off work. I was so happy to see him, hug, kiss, and console him. I felt so sad that he was sad about his friend. We enjoyed each other that night. Caught up on the past two days that we were not in each other's presence. We enjoyed each other so much that I took off from work the next day. We laid around that morning, and by almost noon, decided it was time for us to get up and get our day started.

Even though I missed Flavio and was enjoying catching up and spending time with him, something still was not sitting right with me. I was still curious about him disappearing on me like he had. I decided as soon as I had the chance, I was going to go through his phone for reassurance.

The perfect opportunity presented itself. Flavio was first to get in the shower. Sure enough, when he got in, he left his phone on the nightstand. He had a lock on his phone. But that was not a problem because I had seen him enter his code plenty of times before. He just did not know it. As soon as he got into the shower, I hurried over to his phone and started to investigate as quickly as I could.

While going through his text messages, I noticed this one number was sending all these pictures of a brand-new baby. Not only that, but he was sending the same brand-new baby pictures to other people as well. I made sure I jotted down all the numbers that had the baby pictures, so that when I had the opportunity, I could make a few calls.

It was eating me up to pretend like nothing was wrong after going through his phone. It was hard for me to not question him about what I had seen. Or to even know what I knew after being with him all day laughing, smiling, and loving on each other. But I had to because I had to piece this stuff together.

That night Flavio told me he had to go out of town the next day. He claimed he had to handle some business. I was happy that he was going to be gone, it would give me time to conduct my investigation.

I went to work that day as usual. Flavio said he was going to come by my job and have lunch with me before he got on the road. He brought JJ's Fish and we sat in front of my job and had a nice lunch date. As nice as it had been, he could sense something was wrong with me. He even asked me if something was wrong. Although that was my opportunity to say something, I decided not to. I had to have all my facts straight!

After we ate lunch, we hugged, kissed, and I told him to drive safely. He told me he would see me later that night. I had an appointment that day, so I was already scheduled to get off early. I went to my appointment, hands itching to dial a number, but I had to handle my business. As soon as my appointment was over, the first number I dialed was the number that had been sending those brand-new baby pictures.

A woman answered the phone, and I introduced myself. "Hello, this is Ebony, Flavio's girlfriend. I see you sent him so many pictures of this baby. I want to know whose baby this is and who are you?" She said, "Well, I'm Adriana, and what do you mean Flavio's girlfriend? I'm his baby mama, and those pictures are of our baby that was just born 3 days ago." I was stunned. I sat there thinking to myself, "Wow, Ebony, how could you have allowed something like this to happen? Not AGAIN!!!" I was so disappointed with myself.

As hard as it was for me to do, I pushed my emotions aside and continued the conversation. She and I began sharing stories of our relationship with Flavio, and at the end of our conversation, I told her he was on his way to her now, and good luck with him because he will not be coming back here! I was done.

I did not even call Flavio to confront him about it. There was no point for me to. He lied from the beginning. He knew he had a baby on the way and should have told me. He should have allowed me the courtesy of letting me decide if I still wanted to deal with him. But he did not. He decided for me. He was just another let down.

Surprisingly, I was not even hurt. I was just so mad at myself because I let this man fool me and fool me good. I immediately disconnected the phone services for his phone. I then threw all his belongings in the green dumpster outside.

Afterwards, I handled it like I did all of the other big deals in my life. I followed my one faithful fireproof pattern, and I drank it away.

I started drinking early on Saturday, all while running my weekend errands. I was getting things done all while drinking. I stopped by my girlfriend's house before going home. I sat over there and told her what happened and drank some more. By the time I got ready to go, it was dark outside. I am driving, and all I see is blue and red lights behind me. I was getting pulled over.

Of course, I smelled like liquor, so the police told me to step out of the car and asked me had I been drinking. I told him yes, but like one or two drinks. The officer had me blow in that machine and I blew a .17. I was now taking my second trip down to Sacramento County Jail, and alcohol was the factor. I was so worried about my job, but because this was on a Saturday, I ended up being released on Sunday, and was able to make it to work without my job knowing what happened. Another bullet I thought I dodged.

THE LOCKS

CHAPTER 7

THE LOCKS

never heard from or saw Flavio again. Crazy how I would just send people on their way with no further attachments. My heart was getting darker and darker.

Life carried on, and I now had a second DUI that I had to deal with, all while working and keeping it from my job.

Diablo got out of jail. Lucia told me he had been trying to get in contact with me. I was not dating anybody at the time, so I told her, "What the hell, go ahead and give him my number." He and I started talking again. He expressed to me how hurt he was that I just left him with no explanation or anything. I expressed to him how that life was not for me. He listened to what I had to say and still decided he wanted to date me.

Shortly after having our heart to heart talk, we met up one weekend. That night we had the best night ever. We had so much fun. We started off going bowling. I had not been bowling in such a long time. I felt like a kid again. Afterwards, we went to grab burgers at IN-N-Out, and then ended up at the Sheraton Hotel. I had not had sex in a long time, so what better time than now. I went against my first mind when I first met Diablo and opened myself up to him. We had sex that night, and the next morning went to breakfast. I started making myself believe he was the right one for me because he was showing me such a great time.

After the wonderful night we had, we went on to talk every day for the next week or so. It was like clockwork. I would talk to him every morning with well wishes for a great day, and text messages all throughout the day. Until one morning I did not hear from him. I called him but there was no answer. I was both so lost and confused, but I managed to carry on with my day. I learned from the past that these men can be here today and gone tomorrow. Unfortunately, that was not necessarily the case this time.

Later that evening, I got a call from his uncle. Diablo had been arrested that morning. He tried to run from the police, and they sent the dogs after him. He had been bitten up bad, so his first stop was the hospital.

Finally, after two days, I got the call I had been waiting on from him: "You have a collect call from the San Joaquin County Jail." Of course, I accepted the charges. I was momentarily relieved when I heard his voice. The relief quickly turned into sadness because he sounded like he was in so much pain. At that moment, I decided I was not going to leave him this time. I was going to be that down ass chick that he needed me to be. I went to his court dates and went to visit him as much as I could. He was in a wheelchair, so that weighed even heavier on my heart.

Due to his charges, and the fact that he had priors, it was decided that he had to do prison time. Before he got to his prison sentence, he had to go through reception. When he first got to reception, I did not get to talk to him for about a month. When we finally did talk, I started falling in love with him. I was determined to do everything I could for our relationship. Fortunately, the court decided that they were not going to house him in a prison, but that he could carry out his prison sentence on an ankle monitor for one year.

We were now in a relationship, so he was going to do his sentence right at home with me. I was excited. I did all the paperwork so that this man from the streets that I barely even knew, could move into my home. I had no idea what I was getting myself into. I moved on pure impulse.

I set my house up so nice for him to feel comfortable, and I went into this relationship full speed ahead. I was still working, so while he was home all day, I was working. He would do all the housework which was a real sweet deal for me. All I had to do was work, cook sometimes, and have sex. Life was good.

After about two months of pure bliss, I was on my way home from work, as I approached my house, I saw this woman walking out of the front door of my house. Dressed in these real flimsy clothes, like she was coming to see somebody for a hot date. I could not believe what I was witnessing. Shocked and appalled, I watched this woman scurry to her car. Hop in and pull off.

I immediately got out of my car and went inside. Diablo looked as if he had just woken up, there was a blanket folded on my couch. I knew what had been going on. I went off. I told him he had to go. He swore up and down that the lady was just there to drop something off from his friend. I did not want to hear it. He got on the phone and called his mother. While he was on the phone with his mother, I was on a rampage. I have a real bad mouth when I am upset, and I go to a real dark place. His mom is a Christian woman, and I was going off. I must have said something that touched a nerve because Diablo drew his arm back while on the phone with his mother and socked me in my jaw. Oh, it was on from there. I grabbed the closest thing to me which was a pot and started wailing on him. How dare he put his hands on me. I am far from a punk. I was like, "Come on, let's go, blow for blow with it then."

After things settled down, Diablo still stuck with the story. He continued to proclaim that he was not cheating on me with that lady. I did not believe him. All I could think of was what could possibly be going on at my house while I was gone. I decided that I would set him up just like I had done Flavio. But why? I did not need proof; I had been through this before.

Like I had done before, I added Diablo to my phone line. He was happy he had the latest iPhone just like Flavio had been. But things were different this time. I decided to take things a step further. I went to the spy store and got a recorder and hid it in my house so I could hear everything that was going on in my house while I was away. Instead of me just making this man leave my house, I had set out on a mission to catch him.

Every day thereafter, I went to work stressed. I could not wait to get off and listen to that recorder. I could not wait to match his conversations with the numbers on my phone bill. Just about every day, I sat in my car drinking while listening to what had been recorded while I was away.

This was no longer bliss, but a horrible self-destructive path I was on. The things I heard on that recorder were very saddening. He was talking to a host of other women. He was saying mean things about me to his friends. After all I had done for him. How could he? Finally, one day, I had enough! I called him and told him he had to go. I told him things were not going to work out with us. I was going off, cussing him out. In the midst of my rampage, I called him a bi*** and got off the phone.

When I got home that evening, he did not appear to be going anywhere. He was laying in my bed. I did not feel like arguing anymore, so I got in the bed. We did not speak one word. After I laid there on my back for about 5 minutes, I felt him move as if to get up. The next thing I knew this man had gotten up over me on his knees and had drawn back and punched me extremely hard in my face. It all happened so fast; I could hear ringing in my head. My vision was blurred. I did not understand why this was happening, but his exact words were, "Don't you ever call me a bi*** again."

I was in tears. I got in my car and left my own house. He was on ankle monitoring, so he was not going to leave. I drove away and called my friend Lucia. She did everything she could to try to console me, but there was really nothing she could do.

I did not fight back this time. I was scared. I did not want to call the police because it just was against the "code" I thought we had at the time. I did not realize he broke the code once he hit me. That one hit blackened both of my eyes and caused blood vessels to break in the white of my eye. I could not go to work for two weeks because my face was distorted.

My mom and I had always been close. I went to her house every day, or at least every other day. After a couple of days of me avoiding going to her house, she felt like something was up, so she came to my house. When she saw my face she went off, and she called the police for me. Instead of me admitting to the police that yes, Diablo was the reason why my face looked like that, I told them I fell off my bed. I lied so they would not take him to jail.

I had no idea that going against my mother that day was just the beginning of a traumatic journey. That day was only the beginning of me allowing him the privilege to abuse me. I guess I had proved to him that I was exactly what he wanted. He had me scared to say anything to him in my own house. After he would abuse me, he would make up for it by being sweet as pie. The part I loved so much was when he was sweet to me. It felt like pure bliss again.

Diablo played on my weakness. He knew I was an alcoholic. He knew when I got drunk, my tongue got loose. Diablo knew that I was liable to say anything. He took advantage of this because he used it as an opportunity to put his hands on me.

To make matters worse, I was still drinking while I was dealing with the courts for my second DUI. During the course of things, the courts finally decided that I would serve 6 days in jail to pay for my crime. Instead of having to go to jail, I was going to be allowed to serve the time on an ankle monitor. In preparation for it, I had planned to take time off from work, so my job would not be involved. I was going to do my 6 days and be done.

The night before I was supposed to go get the ankle monitor put on, I was drinking and had drank a lot. I was so used to carrying on with my day after a night of drinking a lot, that I felt fine the next morning. My mom came to take me to get my ankle monitor installed. When I got to the Sheriff's office, they had me blow into a machine before they put the monitor on me. Even though I felt fine, I still had alcohol in my system. When that machine popped, and the Sheriff's office saw that I was under the influence and was already being put on the ankle monitor for a DUI, they opted out of the ankle monitor and took my butt straight to jail.

I let my family and myself down. There was no way now that my job was not going to find out. I spent the worst 6 days of my life in the county. I was on a downward spiral that I never saw myself coming out of. Diablo was still at my house. My mama was going to my house every day to make sure there was no funny business going on. She dared him to act like she could not be there.

My mama remained there for me throughout the entire ordeal. She was there when I was finally released. Because she knew I had not eaten the entire time I was in jail, she had fresh fried chicken sitting in the car waiting for me. I was grateful and ready to get back to life.

I went back to work as I had originally planned. When I got there that morning, I filled out my timecards. The explanation I gave for the time I was off was that I was sick and in the hospital. After turning in my timecards, they called me into a meeting later to confirm that I was in fact sick and in the hospital.

During the meeting I stuck to my story. I told them I had been sick and was in the hospital. Unbeknownst to me at that time, my managers had known otherwise.

They were trying to give me one last chance to be honest.

After they asked me many times the same questions, and me not being willing to tell the truth, they finally told me that they had evidence that I was, in fact, not in the hospital. They had evidence that I was incarcerated. I did not want to take responsibility for lying to them, so I blamed them for setting me up. They already knew where I was. Why make me go through an interrogation?

I was messing up and messing up bad. At that moment I just knew I was about to lose my good State job. Thankfully, instead of me losing my job, I was served with an Adverse Action which meant my pay would be reduced 25% for the next 12 months. This was all because of my dishonesty and fraudulently filling out my timecards. I was sick! The way those managers treated me that day was as if I committed murder, not lied. The truth is I only lied because I did not want them in my business.

Life on my job was a living hell after that. They made coming to work very miserable for me for the length of my employment there. Although it had gotten bad, I still had not accepted alcohol had played the biggest role in my downfall.

LOCK DOWN

CHAPTER 8

LOCK DOWN

I carried on this completely dysfunctional relationship with Diablo for some time. Once he got off ankle monitoring, he continued going to jail left and right. It did not stop. He was in and out of that place, and I was right there with him like a fool. I allowed this man to break my spirit to the point that I honestly did not believe anyone else wanted me.

According to him, I was fat and ugly. He never ever complimented me. Looking back now, I realize he did this because he was just jealous of how fine I really was. He knew if anyone else knew who I really was, I would be gone in a heartbeat. To stop me from leaving, and others discovering the beauty I possessed, he did unimaginable things to me. These things resulted in me losing sight of my self-worth and self-respect. It ultimately caused me to stop loving myself enough to let go of him and leave.

If I had really loved myself enough, I would have left when Diablo first put his hands on me, when I wanted him out of my house. But I did not. Because of it, I endured hellish situations at every turn.

Once Diablo got off his ankle monitor, he left Sacramento and went to stay in the bay area. During that time, we were still seeing each other. So, I would go to the bay area every weekend just to be with him. On one of those weekend trips, I went through his phone. I was mortified when I saw a video of him having sex with somebody on the same couch we would have sex on. Instead of him apologizing, or even taking responsibility for what he had done, he slapped me for going through his phone as if somehow it was my fault.

Despite the fact that the abuse continued even with me living in Sacramento, and him now living in the bay area, I still could not leave him. And I still continued to visit him every chance I got.

Even though Diablo was living in the bay area, he still did not have a job. To support himself, hustling was his thing. One New Year's Eve, I decided to visit him in the bay area. That night we were supposed to be going to Las Vegas with Lucia and Ricardo. I was really excited about stepping out. Unfortunately, my excitement quickly turned to sadness because he claimed his money was not right, and we could not go to Las Vegas anymore.

Diablo wanted me to ride around with him selling dope on New Year's Eve. When I told him I did not want to go, and I wanted to celebrate New Year's instead, he became enraged. He started yelling at me and acting crazy. When I refused to go along and agree with him, he spit in my face. I could not believe it! I was so humiliated that I decided not to stay in the bay area with him. I ended up leaving and driving back to Sacramento on New Year's Eve.

Shortly after that, Diablo ended up moving back in with me. Around that time, it was my birthday, so my best friend took me out to celebrate. We went out to eat, and then went to the Casino. We got home at about 1 am. I was scared to even go into my own house because it was kind of late.

Instead of going inside, I ended up falling asleep in my car. At about 7 am Diablo came out into the driveway and knocked on my car window waking me up. He was being so sweet, asking me why I was in the car. I told him it was because I knew he would be tripping because of how late I had come home, so I ended up falling asleep in the car.

He reassured me he was not tripping. He even urged me to go ahead and come into the house. Still guarded, I go inside with him. As soon as we walked into the house, Diablo started to fill up a pot of water. By now I knew this man. I knew it was not going to just be that easy. I knew there was something he had possibly been thinking of to punish me. Sure enough that pot of hot water came flying towards my head.

Because I was already prepared to deal with whatever punishment he handed out, my reflexes were faster than the pot. I ducked just in time and I began to run out of the door. As I ran as fast as I could, that man kicked me so hard in my behind that he fractured my tailbone. But I did not know my tailbone was fractured at the time because my adrenaline kept me running. Once he caught me in the middle of the street, he poured syrup in my hair. Because I had braids at the time, I had to take them down.

After that day whenever I would sit down, I felt a sharp pain that prevented me from sitting with ease. I went to the doctor. My doctor ended up ordering x-rays. From the x-rays, I found out the reason why I was in so much pain. My tailbone was fractured.

You would have thought that would have been the end of Diablo and my relationship, but it was not. We made-up and he struck again. We were at my friend's house for a party. Apparently, he didn't like how I was interacting with someone at the party. Abruptly he said it was time to go. Without hesitation, I go to get into the car. Immediately we started arguing. While being seated in the driver's seat, he reached over me and opened the passenger door. He then used his feet to kick me out of the car onto the ground.

My friends heard all of the commotion and came outside. They all threatened to whoop his ass if he laid another hand on me. He was not so tough then.

I should have left him then, but I still could not find the strength. In fact, the only time after that when I came close to it, was when I found out he cheated on me once again. I was certain I was leaving him that time. I had had enough of his crap. I was stopped dead in my tracks from leaving when he decided his way of making it up this time was by proposing to me. All I ever wanted was to get married and have a big beautiful wedding, so I forgave him. We were on cloud nine for a few months after the proposal while we planned our wedding. I just knew he was changing because he was doing everything he could to put a smile on my face.

Reality hit me hard when we went on vacation out of the country. He reverted back to his old ways. Instead of doing everything to put a smile on my face, he did the opposite. He acted like the jealous crazy man he had always been.

While there, I was talking to the locals, having an amazing time. I had no idea that instead of him joining in on the fun, he was sitting in the car watching me from afar. At the time, I did not think anything of it. I continued to mingle until he came out of nowhere. I immediately said, "Erik, this is my husband!", because I already knew how this fool was about to act. As soon as I said that, I was immediately slapped down to the ground by Diablo.

To make matters worse and more painful, my knees scraped the ground to the point that they were bleeding.

All of my family, who were also on the trip, ran outside. The locals were ready to kill this man. They did not play around with a man putting his hands on a woman where we were visiting. My mom got the news of what had happened that night, and she called the police all the way from California. The police showed up to my hotel room. All I could think about my mom was "This lady is off the hook, but I love her the most."

I still lied all the way across the ocean. I had to for my safety. My mom was not there. I knew I had to get us home safely. I hated the embarrassment I went through at that time, and my mama too. For my safety, and to keep the peace, I shut up the rest of the trip and acted just like he wanted me to.

Once we returned back to the states, we made up. The wedding was still on. I had the most beautiful wedding planned for us. Our day was going to be amazing. I was sure of it.

Prior to our wedding date (2 weeks to be exact), my brother came to my house unexpectedly. When he arrived, we were right in the middle of a domestic dispute. I asked my brother to leave me be, and to leave my house. Well, my brother knew something was not right, so he refused to leave. Instead of Diablo allowing me to deal with my brother myself, he took it upon himself to go grab his gun and strike my brother across his head with that gun. My poor brother was just trying to see what was going on with his sister. He had no idea he was going to be attacked, and neither did I. At this point I knew I could not marry him. I called off our wedding, but I still did not leave.

The abuse continued to accelerate after that. He hit me in my eye with a Patrón bottle. I ended up in the hospital. Of course, I lied to the doctors and told them something else had happened. My eye ended up being infected and I had to take antibiotics for two weeks to stop it from oozing. You would have thought that this would have been enough for me to leave, but it still wasn't enough.

One evening, Lucia and Ricardo had come down, and Lucia and I were sitting in my driveway in her car talking. Diablo wanted me to come inside. I guess I was not coming fast enough because the next thing I knew, he had come outside to Lucia's car and started cussing me out. I did not argue back, I covered my face because he was acting like he was possessed with demons, and I knew how this could go. I was in the passenger seat and Lucia was in the driver's seat. He did not hit me, but he hocked back the fattest loogie and spit on me.

I told Lucia to drive. She pulled off and started driving. She was scared. He attached himself to the side of her truck some type of way, and was holding my hair and hitting on me at the same time. I just kept saying, "Bit**, knock this mother fu**** off this car. Drive faster!!" She drove faster.

He finally jumped off of the car. Once we got to a safe place to stop, we did. He had torn my shirt and my bra off. I was left naked and shaken up. Luckily, Lucia had clothes in her car so that I could cover myself up. We figured out that night that Diablo had to be on drugs. There was no way any regular human being would have been able to hold on to a car like that—and why was he going off? This man was always going off for no reason. I still did not leave him.

There were countless other encounters of abuse that occurred after the car incident. I still wanted to marry him. I ended up getting pregnant, and because of this, we decided we were going to elope. Crazy, right? I know! He had me all to himself isolated from my friends and family.

Shortly after I found out that I was pregnant, we went to a football game. Instead of him wanting to sit and watch the game with me, he wanted to sit in the car getting high. When I came to the car looking for him, he became enraged. On the ride home, I was going off. I could not understand why he wanted to go to the football game if he was not really going to be at the football game.

We argued more once we got home. That was until he could not take it any longer. That day I had the prettiest longest weave in my hair. I looked really cute. I had been painting a door in our house the day before, so the paint was still in the house. This man took that bucket of paint and doused it on me. Oh, it was on from there! We slipped and slid in that paint as we were fighting. I could not win, but I knew I had to fight back. I took a blow to the face that knocked me on my behind. I ended up making Diablo leave that night by acting as if I was calling the police.

A few days later, I started having these horrible cramps like I was in labor. But knew I could not be because it was not time. I pushed the thought aside and assumed I had gas. But when I squeezed to release it, all this blood started rushing out. I knew that should not have been happening while I was pregnant. I drove myself to the hospital.

I was concerned and shocked to learn my HCG levels were dropping at a rapid rate. I was having a miscarriage. Everything I ever tried to have with this man was blocked by my God. God had given me sign after sign after sign, but this time I was going to listen.

I never had a miscarriage in my life. But due to me hitting the floor coupled with all the stress I was under I was having one. I decided that this time I was going to call the police. He was going to pay for this black eye. He was going to pay for making me lose my baby.

Separating from him, and the loss of my baby, caused me to start having panic attacks. Something I had never experienced. I went through a great deal of depression. Something else I had never experienced. I would lay in bed for days, only leaving my house to go get a bottle of alcohol to soothe the pain. While at home,

I would cry myself to sleep, wake up, and do it all over again.

I shut myself off from the world because I felt so defeated. Defeated in the fact that I defeated myself. Defeated my family. The panic attacks were a constant nightmare. They were uncontrollable, I had to seek medical help just to get through them. When everything became a trigger for me, I started going to therapy.

Even though I was devastated with the end result, what was in store for me would blow my wildest dreams. This was all in God's plan. No matter how hard I tried to make things work, he said "No way. Not today!"

THE KEYS

CHAPTER 9

THE KEYS

While dealing with the mess in my personal life, it drastically affected my work life. Even though my managers already had it out for me, I was giving them more reasons to target and harass me. I did this by not showing up for work, and by having an even nastier attitude when I would show up.

Thank goodness there were advantages in working for the State. Because I was a victim of domestic violence, I was able to transfer from the department I worked in, to another department within the agency with no questions asked. All for my safety. Diablo knew where I worked, I wanted to go to a place where he could not find me. When I requested the transfer, not only did I get it, but I was transferred into a higher paying position.

I was being blessed and still did not even realize it. Even though I was not too fond of management, the team that I worked with was amazing. I had worked with them for so long, we had turned into a family. I cried so hard on my last day, until one of my teammates (who is still one of the people I go to for prayer and encouragement) uttered words I will never forget, "Girl, you will see us. This is your only way out of here. You better wipe your tears and get to getting. You are being blessed in unthinkable ways right now. Wipe your tears and be thankful this all happened. I love you, and I'm rooting for you!"

I started my new position and was greeted by one of my co- workers, who I started at the State with. She had previously moved on and was now working at this location. When she saw me for the first time in a long time, she knew something was not right with me. She could see I had changed. My spirit was so damaged and broken. I was not the person she was used to seeing show up to work jazzy, cute as ever, bubbly, and cheesing from ear to ear. She met me when there was no Diablo.

Out of concern one day, she asked me if everything was ok. I told her yes. She said, "Naw, you're not the same Ebony I know." It was at that moment I realized I had to get back to the woman I used to be. I prayed so hard one night. Harder than I had ever prayed before. I asked God to carry me, and to guide all my footsteps from that point forward. I was ready to turn my life completely over to him. I was taking my life back.

My girlfriend had gotten me a devotional book, and she challenged me to read that book every day. She encouraged me to see how the words resonated with me. I started to pick myself up, and God reminded me I had the keys the whole time to break out of the jail I had built for myself.

I started caring for my appearance again, and started showing up for work every day. I had a great rapport with my manager, and told her I wanted to clean out my personnel file. I wanted to remove all the negative things that were in my file from the previous department. She agreed. I knew, had I stayed in the other department, this wouldn't have never happened.

Unbeknownst to me, upon her receiving me into her department, she never read my file. Now when she read it, she said she was glad she had not previously done so. The person that she saw in front of her that day was not the person my old managers had put in black in white. See how God works! I may not have wanted to go, but he put me exactly where I needed to be.

I started loving myself more and more every day. I realized it really is a much better feeling to sit alone and figure yourself out; something I had never done. I was from one relationship to the next. Taking on other people's drama when, really, I needed to focus on Ebony.

It was not so easy to break out of the jail I built. I still had hiccups. I was still working on getting my driver's license reinstated. I still was an alcoholic, I just was a functioning alcoholic at this point. I drank just enough to still be able to care for my family and perform my job duties.

One night after a night of drinking I decided that I was ok to drive. Well, I was not ok. I ended up falling asleep behind the wheel of the car and crashing my car into another vehicle. I just knew I was going back to jail. The man that was in the car got out. By the grace of God, I was not hurt, and neither was anybody in the other car.

That man put me in the back of his car, and moved my car onto the side of the road. I must have fallen back to sleep because the next thing I knew, I woke up and it was morning time. I was still in the backseat of their car. I had my purse, my phone, and my keys. I remembered what had happened at that moment, but had no idea where I was, or how I had gotten there. My phone was dead, I could not call an uber, so I got out and started walking.

Next thing I knew, these two sweet little old ladies pulled up on the side of me and asked me if I needed a ride. Of course, I said, "yes." They drove me to my house with no questions asked. That was nothing but God, and my guardian angels.

I retraced my steps and found where my car was parked. Got in my car, and drove it home. My car was pretty banged up, but I had enough cash in my savings to get it repaired. I knew God was not just about to keep letting me play with him. So, from that day I went into seclusion. I went dry with no alcohol for a total of six months. I still had work to do. I thanked God for his mercy, and I started praying and meditating and started discovering myself more and more every day.

I now know what makes me happy. I know what makes me sad. I know what makes me angry. Any emotion you could experience, I know why I have it, and how to deal with it.

There is nothing, or anybody, who can take me to the dark place I was once in. Now, I do not drink like I used to. I only drink off the top shelf. Well, we all know top shelf liquor is expensive, right? So, I cannot afford to get drunk. I only will have a drink on special occasions, and it is nothing but the best. This is because I realized I deserve nothing less than the best.

I did the work and went to the classes to get my driver's license back. I now drive without the worry of being pulled over. I also make better choices. If I plan on drinking anywhere besides in my home, I get a ride there and a ride back. I worked too hard to get to where I am today, and I refuse to mess it up for anybody, or through self-sabotage; that's a thing of the past.

Focusing on myself and pouring every ounce of love I had into myself, took me to heights I never thought I would ever reach. I am now well on my way to becoming the manager in my department. I took the good from the greatest managers that saw the greatness in me, and appreciated the bad because it taught me how a manager should not be.

Once I realized I had the keys the whole time, I unlocked every door and broke out the jail I built. I forgave myself for every mistake I made. That was the first step I took on my path to staying free. I did not care what anybody had to say about anything that had happened in my past. God and I were on one accord.

Even though my mom rocked hard with me through all my downfalls, I know I disappointed her in many ways. She would start having flashbacks to those times, and would start going off about things that happened. I was not moved. She did not know it yet, but I was healed from every unthinkable thing that happened in my past. I just knew it was time to show and prove. Lucia even tried to throw daggers at times. She was used to the wild partying drunk friend, and would say things like, "Girl, you need to stop being fake. Why you always acting so happy?" Instead of her embracing my positive changes, she wanted to take me back to that dark place that I left in the past. I just quit dealing with her. Anybody who was not riding my wave, and was not on the same frequency as me, got left in my dust.

Forgiving everyone that I knew wronged me, purified my heart. I realized the demons they possessed were trying to attack me, and I could not be more thankful that God protected me and opened my eyes and purified my heart again. By no means am I perfect, but I know my intentions always have been and will always be pure.

Changing my mindset really changed my life. Remembering that I deserved nothing but the best, allowed me to sleep peacefully at night. Remaining grounded in prayer, and maintaining my daily spiritual rituals, gave me peace, and that peace allowed me to press forward every single day.

Yes, I went through trials. Yes, I went through tribulations. Yes, I was broken. Yes, I went in circles worried about what I looked like from the outside looking in. Yes, I allowed others to tear me down. I was broken and scared. No longer a jailbird, I put the pieces back together and licked my wounds. I started looking within and started living unapologetically Ebony's true self. I remembered who I was, and simply replaced my crown with a bigger, brighter, shinier one—with all the finest diamonds, gems, and bezels! This is only the beginning. Recreated, QueenE.

ABOUT THE AUTHOR

Ebony A.N. Smith, received her education at Los Rios Community College. She is a woman who has had her fair share of dead-end relationships and knows what it is to "settle", get lost, forget your worth, and blame others for your shortcomings. She decided to share her story to encourage women to never settle and always remember their worth. Her decisions have shown her that even the strongest get weak, but when you change your mindset, take accountability, and pray, you can still walk in your purpose no matter how hard you fall.

When Ebony is not working for the State of California, she enjoys spending time with her three beautiful children. Ebony and her family currently reside in Sacramento, CA.

CONNECT WITH EBONY

www.ebony-smith.com

FB: @Ebony Smith

Instagram: @mzebeezee

Email: breakingoutthejail@gmail.com

If you are a victim of domestic violence or know someone who needs help, The National Domestic Violence Hotline is available 24/7/365. Their highly trained advocates are available to talk confidentially with anyone experiencing domestic violence, seeking resources or information, or questioning unhealthy aspects of their relationship. Contact them @ 1-800-799-SAFE(7233). This statement was pulled directly from their website https://www.thehotline.org on 06/25/2020.

Made in the USA
Monee, IL
11 October 2020

44314237R00069